Succeeding in China

The Lessons Learned Series

Learn how the most accomplished leaders from around the globe have tackled their toughest challenges in the Harvard Business Press *Lessons Learned* series.

Concise and engaging, each volume in this series offers fourteen insightful essays by top leaders in industry, the public sector, and academia on the most pressing issues they've faced. The *Lessons Learned* series also offers all of the lessons in their original video format, free bonus videos, and other exclusive features on the 50 Lessons companion Web site: **www.50lessons.com/china**.

Both in print and online, *Lessons Learned* contributors share surprisingly personal and insightful anecdotes and offer authoritative and practical advice drawn from their years of hard-won experience.

A crucial resource for today's busy executive, *Lessons Learned* gives you instant access to the wisdom and expertise of the world's most talented leaders.

Other books in the series:

⊰ **LESSONS LEARNED** ⊱

Succeeding in China

LES50NS

www.50lessons.com/china

Boston, Massachusetts

Printed in the United States of America
14 13 12 11 10   5 4 3 2 1

Library of Congress Cataloging-in-Publication Data

Succeeding in China.
      p. cm. — (Lessons learned)
   ISBN 978-1-4221-3987-5 (pbk. : alk. paper)
   1.   Marketing—China.   2.   Success in business—
China. 3.   Investments, Foreign—China. I.   Fifty
Lessons (Firm)
   HF5415.12.C5S83 2010
   658'.0490951—dc22

                        2009045619

In partnership with 50 Lessons, a leading
provider of digital media content, Harvard
Business Press is pleased to offer *Lessons
Learned*, a book series that showcases the
trusted voices of the world's most experienced leaders. Through the power of personal storytelling, each book in this series
presents the accumulated wisdom of some
of the world's best-known experts and offers
insights into how these individuals think,
approach new challenges, and use hard-won
lessons from experience to shape their leadership philosophies. Organized thematically
according to the topics at the top of man-
agers' agendas—leadership, change management, entrepreneurship, innovation, and
strategy, to name a few—each book draws
from 50 Lessons' extensive video library
of interviews with CEOs and other thought
leaders. Here, the world's leading senior

A Note from the Publisher

executives, academics, and business thinkers speak directly and candidly about their triumphs and defeats. Taken together, these powerful stories offer the advice you'll need to take on tomorrow's challenges.

As you read this book, we encourage you to visit **www.50lessons.com/china** to view videos of these lessons as well as additional bonus material on this topic. You'll find not only new ways of looking at the world, but also the tried-and-true advice you need to illuminate the path forward.

⊰ CONTENTS ⊱

Contents

Succeeding in China

Living in China

Tom Doctoroff

CEO, J. Walter Thompson for Greater China

THE FIRST THING I noticed when I got
off the plane were facial expressions that
were alive, eyes that sparkled, eyes that were
curious. Then when I was getting into a taxi,
the driver wanted to practice his English.
And when I got into the hotel, people just
had this hope for the future, this optimism,
and this stick-to-itiveness, and the ambition for a better tomorrow—not just for
themselves, but for their families. That

moved me. So the first thing I noticed—and the reason why I knew I was going to like it— is that senses were alive and eyes sparkled.

When you first come off the plane and then go into your first experience in a Chinese city, whether it be Shanghai or Beijing, you either like it or you don't like it. You are either besieged by the crushing inefficiency and the soul-sapping conformity of the public sector—of the old China, the imploding China—or you are inspired by the ambition and the sparkle and the dynamism of the new China and the rising China. So the first thing about living in China is your own gut check. You either like it, or you don't like it.

If you do not like it, get back on the plane, because the one thing that Chinese are sensitive to is any cultural arrogance, any whiff of racism, of judgment. If they don't feel that you have a fondness for them, they will turn against you. On the other hand, if they sense that you have genuine affection for their ambition—for their liveliness, for their humor, for their general sparkle, for their incredible leaps of progress and their goals to stand shoulder-to-shoulder astride the globe next to the United States as the next superpower—if that moves you, they will sense it. So the first lesson is, take your gut check, and know whether this is going to be swimming upstream for you or whether it's going to be swimming with the current.

Assuming that you do like China and you are fond of the Chinese people, then you have to realize that this is a society in which safety guarantees minimal danger. So there is a lot of passivity, particularly in the public sector. That means, though, that you can shake the structure. When you are faced with a blank face—I mean, the first words that any foreigners learn is *mei banfa*. *Mei banfa* literally means "there is no way": no way to handle, no method to handle. It is an excuse for absolute passivity and blank expressions that go nowhere. The only way around that is to shake the tree. This is not like Japan or even Thailand, fundamentally Buddhist cultures or Taoist cultures, where people take genuine comfort in regressing to the mean. Here in China, people are afraid of getting in trouble by their superiors.

So if you, for example, are confronting a delayed airline, and you want information—I'm sorry, this might be politically incorrect, but—I feel that you have to demand, perhaps with a fist banging on the counter, to have somebody call up the gate and find out specifically what the problem is. If you're faced with rude service in the restaurants, then you have to make your displeasure known in a way that makes people fear that their retreat to the hierarchy, retreat to what their role is—the minimal definition of what they should be doing, from a service perspective—is in fact a liability. You have to turn the hierarchy against them. If people think that you basically understand them and that you basically can make a joke and have a wink about what you're doing, that solves a lot. If they feel understood at the same time you're shaking the tree, or you are able to crack a joke in the meantime, then I think that works pretty well.

Living in China

It really comes down to personality. Do you have a natural empathy? Chinese have the word *tong qing*, but that literally means "sympathy." When I say *empathy*, I mean the feeling for what is motivating people and whether you can project and convey that so you're never coming across as arrogant, but instead as just somebody who wants to move things forward. Because they want to move things forward, too. They don't like stagnation.

Living in China is really a very personal thing where there's no golden rule except "know your gut."

TAKEAWAYS

⛩ When you first arrive in China, take a gut check to know whether living there is going to be swimming upstream for you or whether it's going to be swimming with the current.

⚏ The contrast in China is such that you are either besieged by the crushing inefficiency and the soul-sapping conformity of the old, imploding China or you are inspired by the ambition and the sparkle and the dynamism of the new and the rising China.

⚏ Although there is a lot of passivity in China, if people think that you basically understand them and if you can make a joke and have a wink about what you're doing, shaking up the status quo can successfully move things forward.

———◆◆◆———

Entering the Chinese Market

———◆◆◆———

Eric Tarchoune

Managing Director, Dragonfly Group

I STUDIED CHINESE a long time ago, when I lived a little bit in Taiwan and Singapore before I moved to Beijing in the early '90s. When I moved, I was working as a project manager doing market intelligence for a Scandinavian company. Once, I was asked by the general manager to study the market and set up three profit centers. This company was selling drilling and transportation equipment for mines, for civil engineering projects. We were selling to ministries and local engineering bureaus under the umbrella of ministries, kind of dealing with state-owned companies. So I traveled to part of China, in the west, because our clients were in remote areas.

Finally, I decided to set up offices in three cities. One was Chengdu in Sichuan, the capital of Sichuan province. The other ones were Wuhan in Hubei Province and in Xi'an. I thought those were the best locations in terms of how to find local talent and how to set up and operate a company. I traveled quite a lot prior to establishing these offices, alone and with cash in my pocket to start registration processes, rent premises, and buy the usual, required equipment for operating an office.

It was like learning the ropes when I started dealing with the local authorities, first because these places—it was the early to mid-'90s—were not so open yet. The big cities on the coastline, like Beijing, Shanghai, Guangzhou, and some other

Entering the Chinese Market

ones were okay. But in these places where I was establishing offices, you hardly had foreign companies. Most of the time, when I was meeting with officials—I was quite young—they were surprised I could speak Chinese. And they showed a certain level of interest: why is this young foreigner coming here to build a business? I was also quite self-confident. I knew I could do it, it was a challenge, and I loved it. It was a very interesting experience.

As a consequence of meeting with these people, I was invited to speak in Chengdu, in front of the vice governor. I met the vice governor, and I even had my picture on the investment guide for Sichuan in the mid-'90s. It was kind of funny. I really learned a lot through that experience, because it was difficult. It was a China I didn't know. It taught me to be patient, to develop lots of personal connections. It was important for me to understand that in order to succeed, you have to develop personal connections, especially connections with the local bureaucracy. I brought some gifts, and I spent a lot of time with the officials.

Succeeding in China

When setting up a company at that time, all the regulations were in Chinese, so I had to translate everything to report to the headquarters in northern Europe. I was so happy I could speak, read, and write Chinese, especially reading Chinese. Otherwise, there would have been no way for me to be able to succeed in that challenge. It is so interesting, because you have lots of internal regulation. They call it *Nei Bu* in Chinese. So some people one day say something to you, and another day it's a different thing. And if you ask, "Why? Do you have any supporting documents?" they say, "No, it's confidential. It's not open to outsiders." You really have to trust them. But actually, nothing bad happened. It was a very interesting experience.

The conclusion to that experience is, if you're in China—it's valid in some other countries, but it's even more important in China—act like the Chinese. Adapt yourself and follow the rules, even if they are not written on the wall. Learn by doing and learn by exchanging with people.

TAKEAWAYS

- When you are entering the Chinese market, it's important to be patient and develop many personal connections, especially within the local bureaucracy.

- The ability to read and write the native language where you're doing business is a tremendous advantage to overcoming challenges.

- In foreign markets, adapt yourself, learn by doing, and follow the rules, even if they're not explicitly stated.

Take Risks to Enter New Markets

Carl H. Hahn

Former President, Volkswagen

A BIG DECISION for me in 1982 was whether to go to China or not. None of our competitors was willing to go to China, as they didn't give China any future. China was in the aftermath of a cultural revolution, which was probably one of the most destructive periods of Chinese history, having set back the country, having destroyed the treasures of the country, and having isolated, discriminated, and prosecuted the Chinese intellectual elite. You couldn't do more stupid things or destructive things in a shorter time than what we had seen in the final days of Mao.

With Deng Xiaoping, a completely new period had started. I had heard about it. When I met the people of the Chinese government and of the Communist Party of China, I was so impressed with their determination and their honesty to make a real change. I thought also at the time that China, after the cultural revolution, after the Great Leap Forward—which was also something that, of course, did cost thirty million Chinese their lives—I thought that China was ready for a radical change for the better. Some very significant elements confirmed me in my opinion.

I found that the new Chinese leaders, who mostly had studied in Moscow University or the Saint Petersburg University, had

sent their children to Great Britain, to
Oxford or Cambridge, or to the United
States, to the Massachusetts Institute of
Technology or Harvard Business School,
and so on. They were determined to have a
new long-term policy. They had seen the
results of a market economy, of a capitalist
economy. They realized the challenges and
also the risks involved. I was convinced that
these were people you could work with. For
my counterparts, on the other hand, the
automobile was a great symbol of industrial-
ization. But also, nothing is more desired,
whether you are poor or rich, than the own-
ership of a car. This car has an enormous
political value, and it was, for the Chinese
government, an important project. They
were following up extremely closely.

Consequently, I had many, many discus-
sions with the Chinese government, with
Xiu Long Ji, for instance, whom I consider
one of the greatest economic leaders of the
twentieth century, compared to our Ludwig
Erhard in Germany, whom we credit right-
fully with having brought Germany back on

the path to a free-market economy and to our successful reentry into the world economy. Li Peng was another one, and Yan Su Min, this highly cultured man who had such enormous vision and became such a strong influence also in international politics for China. All told, I found a fantastic group of leaders who were determined and, in my opinion, on absolutely the right course for China.

Consequently, we decided we would start in China. It was the smallest project I think we ever started. First-year production was seventeen hundred automobiles: nothing. Nevertheless, I told the Chinese government with conviction that I considered this the most important project of our company for the years to come.

TAKEAWAYS

- When you are analyzing whether or not to enter the Chinese market, it is important to understand the country's history.

- A country's leadership and its intentions for the future are major components of how successful its markets will be.

- Aligning your business with the needs and objectives of the government can increase your chances for success.

Choose the Right Mix of Local and Foreign Partners

Burkhard Welkener

Former Managing Director,
Volkswagen Motor Group

I TRIED FROM the beginning to persuade local German medium-sized suppliers to come to China. At the time, that was very, very difficult, because they believed the risk was too high for them. They might lose a million deutschmarks; at that time they were fearful it would bankrupt their companies. So I said, can we pull a special team of different suppliers together as one group, and go overseas? But in this case, I failed as well.

Then I tried to persuade them, saying, "OK, if you come in now, like Volkswagen, with a very small group, you can build up the market; you can build up your teams and your partnerships with the Chinese suppliers."

But it was, at the time, very, very difficult. And only a few, small companies made the leap and said, "OK, I would like to play with this investment of one million German deutschmarks; maybe I will lose, maybe not, but I can take it."

Most of them—not everybody, but most of them—were successful following the big increase of volume in the development of the Chinese automotive market. And now, ten or twenty years later, the others realize that maybe it's too late. And it is too late.

The Right Mix of Partners

They say, "Okay, what can I do? Can I take my used equipment?"

I say, "No you cannot, because today the Chinese like to have the most modern technology available in the market. So you cannot. You missed the chance. Twenty years ago, you could ship old technology to China to train the people, to train the suppliers, but today you cannot."

The most modern technology is necessary, and they, of course, fear, when they bring the most modern technology from overseas to China, that the Chinese will copy very fast, and then the Chinese will bring the products back to their own mother countries more cheaply. That's the first fear.

The second fear is that they say, "I don't have a partner in China. I cannot afford green grass production. I cannot go and start from scratch without knowing the partners, without knowing the customers' demand," and so on.

So then we said, "Okay, we are prepared to start any corporation you like. We have so many different areas of businesses; it's easy for us to cooperate with a steel or sheet metal company, with a plastic company, even with wind crafts, or whatever. So we are prepared within our group to be a partner."

That's the way we discuss it now. When companies from Germany come and ask for an entry into the Chinese market, we try to find a partner for them. But it's much more difficult because of the competition. Sometimes I believe the competition in China— the cost reduction pressure—is much higher than in Europe.

TAKEAWAYS

- ◁ You can mitigate some risk by entering the Chinese market with partners who are willing to collaborate with you.

- ◁ In more mature markets, such as the automotive industry, China requires the most modern technology available.

The Opportunities and Challenges of Working in China

Michael Dell

Chairman and CEO, Dell

interviewed by Mark Thompson

Mark Thompson: WHEN YOU THINK about where you're expanding and mapping a broader strategy for the operation, would China be another one of those places where it's obvious that they've been a supply chain and now they're also a market? Could you talk about the potential for China?

Michael Dell: China is our third-largest market. We've had seven years of 45 percent compounded annual growth in China. We have two factories in China. We're heading rapidly into the west, into the tier three, four, five, six, and seven type of cities, and we're penetrating those as well.

There is uniqueness in every market, and China has a scale that is unparalleled. We're going after it. You can find just about every principal activity of Dell occurring in China—from IT development to research and development, to manufacturing, to sales service support. You pretty much have all aspects of the company operating there.

MT: How would you advise entrepreneurs who want to break into that market and think about it both from the back office or the development side as well as a consumer market?

Opportunities and Challenges

MD: We find some differences there, but when you talk about the way larger organizations work, whether they're global companies or the large Chinese national companies, it's not dramatically different from the way large companies work in other countries. When you get in a consumer market, that could be a bit different because of credit and the scale and distribution. And, of course, you have many different Chinas. You have the cities; you have the rural. You have all these tier-three through tier-seven cities. There's a multitude of opportunities.

One thing we found in China is that customers really value relationships. So when Dell comes and we say we want to have a relationship, we show up and we stay. We want to understand more about their business and more about their needs. That works. It actually works everywhere. I think it's a universal belief system, that people want to have relationships.

MT: Right. It is a ubiquitous principle of all cultures. Certainly, understanding that there are so many differences between the different Chinas is a bit like understanding the different markets that you have around the world, within the U.S. and Europe. Is there a description you can make of a particular visit that had impact on you when you realized that things had changed in terms of serving China?

MD: We've had to do things differently there to achieve the success. First, it's not for the faint of heart, because there are a lot of things that are sort of changing and unpredictable. I remember at one point—this was very early on in our China experience—we'd built this brand-new factory. A bunch of guys from some government agency showed up, and they had a bunch of papers. They said we couldn't build computers from this factory anymore; it said so there on their papers. This is what we were told in the translation. So we asked what they meant. We called over the mayor, and these guys are fighting and arguing. Two hours later, it's all solved—not a problem anymore.

Opportunities and Challenges

That was the kind of thing that was happening quite a bit in China, just an unpredictable, almost chaotic environment where you had to be ready for anything. And because it was evolving so quickly, they were making up the rules as they went along.

TAKEAWAYS

- ⛉ Because consumer markets vary from rural areas through different tiers of cities, there is a multitude of opportunities in China.

- ⛉ Understanding their business and their needs demonstrates to your customers that you value a relationship with them.

- ⛉ The Chinese market is not for the faint of heart; you need to be ready for anything.

Losing Face

John Northen

Former General Manager, JW Marriott Hotel
Shanghai and Marriott Executive Apartments

YOU DON'T WANT people to be in a
situation where they lose face. There are
two parts, really. There's the idea of losing
face and the idea of maintaining a good
face, having something to be proud of—
either a project that you've been involved
in or perhaps a building that you own. You
want to have the biggest, the best. This is all
about gaining face and ensuring a very good

side. Losing face is the opposite, where you perhaps made a decision—you maybe then change your mind—but you don't want to retract that. You want to find another solution to come around so that you don't actually have to admit you made a mistake.

We opened this hotel about three years ago, and we have altogether 350 bedrooms and 250 apartments, so a total of about 600 keys. We purchased for the hotel, using a local partner, a lot of artwork. Every room had roughly four pieces of artwork. After the hotel was built and ready to open, the partner, a local owning company, did an inventory of everything in the rooms. They came back to us after about ten days and suggested that we should look at the artwork inventory, because a lot of pieces seemed to be missing. They gave us some more detail and said that, yes, based on their calculations, 600 paintings were missing in total from the rooms. Presumably, in their understanding, they had been stolen. Somebody had gone to the rooms and removed 600 paintings.

Losing Face

We went into all 600 rooms, and in every room, there was no evidence—no holes in the wall, no marks where all the fittings would have been for these paintings. We went back and questioned them. They said no. They double-checked, and they were convinced that 600 paintings were missing from the building. We did a lot more investigation and checked the receiving records, and everything seemed to tally. We couldn't understand where it had gone wrong.

Eventually, we went back to the local partner, the owning company, and said, "What we've realized is, it's the interpretation of artwork. In fact, there are in the rooms three paintings and one mirror, which is also in a frame that is included in the total."

I was quite new to China; I didn't really understand this. We kept approaching the subject and saying, no, we can prove that actually it is a mistake, because there are mirrors and paintings under the heading of artwork.

They said, "No, it's actually supposed to be paintings, so you're missing six hundred paintings."

This went on for about three months, and every time we tried to approach the subject, we heard "no." They knew that they were right and we were wrong.

The solution to this was quite complicated. We had to go back to the vendor who supplied the artwork. We asked him to give us a credit note for paintings that had been returned, deduct it from the invoice, and provide us with a separate invoice for the mirrors that had subsequently been delivered.

We went back to the owning company and said, "You're absolutely right. There were six hundred paintings missing, and we have received a credit note. Now we've bought mirrors instead."

Everyone was happy. They could marry up their records; they didn't have to admit making a mistake.

We always avoid putting people on the spot, asking people to make a snap decision.

Losing Face

Once they've made a decision, if later they want to retract that for whatever reason, it's quite difficult. A lot of the time, you'll be given very subtle comments. You'll be asked, "Would you mind checking the inventory of something?" Generally, there's something behind that. People would not ask you to do something for no reason at all. There will always be some reason why they want you to do something. It's very important to look out for even the smallest, subtlest hints. Make sure that you clearly understand what the issue is. Dig a bit deeper, if necessary, and make sure that you keep coming back to that point. It's important to pick up on clues.

When somebody will not back down from a certain position, the other thing that we learned is, what other ways are there of solving the problem? Is there another way of going about it so that you can find a win-win situation? That's something that is very important as well.

TAKEAWAYS

- ⚔ Avoid putting people on the spot by asking them to make a snap decision since, once a decision is made, it is very difficult to retract it without losing face.

- ⚔ Pay attention to comments and questions, which may be subtle hints to underlying issues that are not directly stated.

- ⚔ When someone will not back down from a certain position, it is important to find a win-win approach to solving problems.

The Three Imperatives of Doing Marketing in China

Tom Doctoroff

CEO, J. Walter Thompson for Greater China

THESE ARE A FEW of the observations or lessons that I see regarding three imperatives of doing marketing in China. The first one, which is probably a no-brainer, is that many people overestimate the affordability of many objectives. You hear lots of figures bandied around that the middle class is anywhere from 100 to 150 million people. But you have to remember all the time that this is a very penny-pinched middle class. The key challenge for multinational companies coming in is to understand how products fit into middle-class life and then to shift their position accordingly.

For example, one of the key imperatives of charging a price premium—and as we all know, price premiums are the root of all happiness and the lack thereof is a downward descent into the commoditization spiral—is that you charge a premium for goods that are publicly consumed. That means that if people see you consuming something in public, you're willing to pay more money for it.

Pizza Hut, for example, would never be able to survive just as an in-home delivery. They first start off as pizza parlors, where families can go and project their new-generation status. In fact, Häagen-Dazs has done the same thing, not focusing on in-home consumption. Starbucks has come in, not focusing on microsites within the urban landscape, but instead, the stores are much bigger and the menus are much broader, so people come in there almost in a new-generation, tribal sense to project their new-generation identity. All of this can command quite a price premium.

But as soon as you go into the home, things are very, very cheap. Even in Shanghai, most of the brands are local brands—the Haiers, Changhongs, and the TCLs—because they offer a low price and a basic price-value equation. The key rule for increased profitability is to charge a premium for publicly consumed goods.

A corollary to all of this is you can't just have high margin in China. China is a market where you need scale, too. That's the holy grail of marketing in China—having both margin and scale.

For example, Colgate came into the market with a two-dollar tube of toothpaste, offering a benefit of total oral care, which is pretty sophisticated. People aren't going to pay that much for toothpaste. What Colgate did was lower their cost of goods. They also lowered the price of other subline variants, like Colgate Herbal and Colgate Strong, reducing the cost by about 50 percent. Now their market share is around 25 percent, including the premium brand. So the premium brand now has about 3 percent, but the other two have about 20 percent, or 20 percent plus. P&G as well—for all of its products—has a brand image leader, which is expensive, and that's what they're using to generate advertising and image, but then they reconfigure the portfolio so that, again, it's stretched down and stretched out.

Don't charge too high a price, number one. Number two, make sure that you have public display and that you charge a premium for public display. Number three, make sure that your portfolio of goods within a brand is stretched, so that you have both an aspirational image leader on the one hand, but on the other hand, you are having an array of products that is affordable for a much more mass premium consumer.

TAKEAWAYS

- ⚔ A multinational company coming into China must understand how its product fits into the life of the Chinese middle-class consumer and adjust its price points accordingly.

- ⚔ The key rule for increased profitability is to charge a premium for publicly consumed goods.

- ⚔ Make sure your product portfolio includes an image leader as well as an array of products that are more readily affordable to the masses.

Developing Economies Call for Decisive Change

Yuehong Fu

General Manager, Golden Resource
New Yansha Mall

SHOULD WE DEVELOP large-scale shopping malls? How many shopping malls should we develop? This question depends on the overall condition of the economic environment. From the experience of Europe and especially the United States, per-capita GDP should reach at least $10,000 before the initial development of the shopping mall industry. In Beijing, the GDP is $8,000, already approaching the level of development necessary for the construction of shopping malls. In other words, it's a very early stage of development.

At this point, in order to run a shopping mall, you must be very careful and choose large cities with strong economies, comprehensive municipal infrastructures, and relatively high incomes. At the same time, you should also select an appropriate district in the city to construct the mall. We had some concerns regarding overall economic development. We were lucky enough to open the mall years before the Beijing Olympic Games. The Chinese economy has been continuously growing since, and we are glad to have taken advantage of this period of accelerated development. It was our good fortune.

Decisive Change

At the time, we were worried that should an economic slowdown occur, it would inevitably impact such a big shopping mall. Decreased income and lack of confidence in the economy will cause people to reduce their levels of consumption. That was one big concern. Another concern was whether or not we could attract enough shops in order to open such a large-scale shopping mall. Could we prepare at least 90 percent of shops to open for business by our opening day? Could these shops survive? Could they all make money in the mall? Would customers accept the brands we had already introduced? All these problems were solved step by step.

Shops that customers do not like will inevitably have poor performance. Of course, they will be replaced. Every year, on average, we replaced about a hundred shops. It's a lot of hard work, but all necessary to run a shopping mall well. When we opened our mall, the west of Beijing was not a mature business district. This peripheral area was newly developed, and residences around the shopping mall were newly built. Thus, there were not sufficient numbers of customers from the areas surrounding the mall. Though we had done a good job attracting shops prior to our opening and had achieved a 90 percent occupancy rate, we obviously didn't have enough customers. The sales of our tenants were below their expectations.

It was a tough challenge for the shopping mall. Could we continue operations? Could we maintain stability? Could we manage to increase sales from the bottom of a valley to normal status or even better? We were under immense pressure at that time. After analysis of the shops, the market, and our own capabilities, we firmly decided to offer tenants a 25 percent discount on their rent vis-à-vis the original rental contracts. Now, this decision might lead to a decrease of tens of millions in rents. But to respond to the future market challenges and ensure survival of the shopping mall, we made the decision in a really short period of time.

Decisive Change

The decision effectively settled the shops, and consequently, the number of customers slowly increased. In the second year, we reduced the discount of rents to 10 percent. For the third year, we returned to the level of rent stipulated by the original agreements. In this way, we shared risk with the shops and managed to navigate this period of market development together with them. The decision was definitely the correct one. However, it was a great challenge to us at that time.

TAKEAWAYS

- You can learn a great deal about market timing in China by looking at how markets developed in Europe and in the United States.

- Sharing economic risk with businesses who are consuming your services is an effective strategy for weathering short-term downturns.

- Developing markets require creative and innovative measures in order to achieve success.

—◆—

Evolving Your Business Model

—◆—

Dr. William K. Fung

Group Managing Director,
Li & Fung Group

LI & FUNG is a very old company. We've had one hundred years of history. Most people think that it's been fair sailing for one hundred years, but that's obviously not the case. I could tell you that there are very critical junctures in the history of the company where, if we hadn't reinvented ourselves, we would be history.

One of the things that my father's generation did successfully was to be an intermediary between buyers from the United States, Europe, and Japan, and manufacturers of labor-intensive consumer products in the developing parts of the world. By the time my brother, Victor, and I got back to Hong Kong in 1972–73, cracks were already beginning to appear in this business model to the extent that the world was getting smaller, with people now flying around more easily. The language barrier was no longer a barrier.

Not only that, but if you think about it, in just the process of putting together a buyer and the right factory, most countries had free services to do that kind of matching. Hong Kong, for example, has its Trade Development Council, which does that. Every country you remember in the '70s and '80s wanted to promote their exports, and every country had some kind of an institutionalized, probably free, service.

Evolving Your Business Model

Adopting the role of intermediary and saying, "I know the market and I can introduce you to the right factories"—those days were obviously either over or there was very low value added.

Obviously, what we had to do was change. That's why we developed this whole concept, which, later on, people gave the name *supply-chain management*. The idea was not to offer a brokering service; the idea was that you managed the whole process. At first, we started with the idea. We looked past the factories and went to the raw-material source because the raw materials, by that time, could be in a different place. What happened with the globalization process was that production didn't just jump from country to country. It was a process where the labor-intensive portions of manufacturing were first moved to the place where labor was cheaper.

Let's say that instead of Hong Kong, they moved labor to Taiwan, but the denim fabric was still from Hong Kong, where the textile mills were. Then later on, when

Taiwan outgrew day labor—it got too expensive—the labor moved to Indonesia, but the fabric mills were in Taiwan. So there was an extended, at that time, supply chain.

What Li & Fung did was say that, hey, a big determinant of the cost is not just the labor; it's also the fabric and the raw materials—the whole thing. We developed this whole concept to what we were doing, which, later on, academics called supply-chain management, and it was on a global scale. The unfortunate thing about this is that we now call it supply-chain management. The problem with supply-chain management is that it is such an overused concept that every truck driver thinks he's a supply-chain manager. Li & Fung actually manages very complex supply chains—extending over many parts of the world—and we seek out the best place to source a certain component or raw material. Then we bring it all together and assemble it in the best place.

For example, we have a stuffed toy that talks. For a long time, this stuffed toy product was made in Korea, where they had the

machinery and the plush fabric. From that
we evolved into a situation today where we
say, Okay, Korea still has the best fabric, the
plush fabric—if you want the fabric to last
and so on, you get it from Korea. Now we're
bringing that plush fabric into Shanghai,
near Shanghai, where we're doing the
sewing, and we're customizing the sound
chip—the talking part of it—in Taiwan. We
bring it all together, and now we have the
best product because we're taking the best
of breed. We're building supply chains
that bring it together to produce the best
product.

That's the evolution, and it's not a simple
brokering job of saying that, hey, here's a
customer, let me find a factory. The whole
concept of managing the supply chain
rather than managing just the brokering
function between the factory and the buyer
has evolved, and now Li & Fung is known
as one of the world's leading supply-chain
management companies.

TAKEAWAYS

- It is necessary to evolve your business model over time, to accommodate changes in your market and in the world.

- The successful evolution of one company's business model has the potential to create a new industry or synthesize existing industries in new ways.

- Supply-chain management uses the most cost-effective means and locations to successfully coordinate the sourcing of raw materials and material components with the manufacturing processes that combine those components into finished products.

Create an Environment to Retain Your People

Eric Tarchoune

Managing Director, Dragonfly Group

IN CHINA, family is very important. So people, when they're joining a corporation, they expect the corporation to treat them a little bit like part of the family, to re-create this family bond with them. Also, one of the key issues today is the war for talent—the war for talented individuals in China.

I didn't have to force myself, because I am kind of a people person. When I set up my first business, and the same for the rest, I wanted it to have team members. I don't consider the people working with me as staff. To me, there's a very big difference when you say the people are working for me or with me. To me, they're working with me; they're not working for me. They are really team members; they are really part of the family. And I enjoy working with them, and they enjoy working with me because we have developed a bond.

Of course, it's easier when you are the owner of your business, when you're here for the long term, and when you enjoy the place and even the culture you're living in. But even for larger corporations, even for newcomers, if you are really interested in developing a relationship with people, it's a good way to retain them. In order to retain talent, we decided to—and we also advise our

Retain Your People

clients to—develop this caring for people. There are many ways to care for people. We developed some flexible working time. Some people flex because we're working on projects most of the time, so there is the beginning and the end, but in the meantime, people manage their time the way they want. We just have a deadline to be respected.

People are key assets. We acknowledge this—and lots of companies are acknowledging this in the world today—because there's a lack of talented people in every market. In emerging markets, it's even more acute. If you want to keep the people with the right skills and with the right behavior, it's a personal investment. The cost of losing people is very high in every market, and it's even higher in China because the temptations are more significant: there are lots of new businesses, lots of companies are pouring in, and the salaries keep rising. When you start to implement this, let's say, caring type of corporate culture, you stand more chances to retain six, seven, or eight out of ten people.

It's a link with the individual; it's a link with the top management and how they see the people. Do they see people as an asset or as a liability? If they see people as an asset, they will implement policies to keep people happy. And if they see people as a cost, people will sense it and leave.

TAKEAWAYS

- In China, family is very important, so when people join a corporation, they expect the corporation to treat them a little bit like part of the family.

- In order to retain talent—people with the right skills and the right behavior—you must develop ways of caring for people.

Retain Your People

- If a company's management sees people as a cost and does not implement policies to keep them happy, people will sense it and leave.

Loyalty to Employees

John Northen

Former General Manager,
JW Marriott Hotel Shanghai and
Marriott Executive Apartments

WE'RE VERY KEEN to generate, build, and instill loyalty in all of our associates. What we've learned in China is that people are very loyal and can be very loyal. The loyalty that we've experienced here is more to an individual than to a corporation. We're quite lucky in one respect, in that Marriott is a family company and has the person with the name Marriott as head of the organization. An example of where loyalty works against you is if you are employing people and the main benefit you're selling to the employees, to your associates, is the benefits of being part of a corporation, even if it's a global benefit. That's less meaningful, in our experience, than having more of a family.

If you go in our hotel here to what we call the back of the house—the area where the staff arrive in the morning and spend most of the time when they're in between working, going down for meals, for training, and so on—we used to put a lot of posters and displays on the wall just using the name Marriott. What we've done now is change this around. We have more pictures of the history of our company, showing the founder when he first began his business— actually, it was his father who began the business in 1927, so there are photographs of him and his wife, then the son, and then the next generation. People can relate to the face behind the name.

One of the difficulties in China is that there is quite a high turnover of labor in every industry, not only the hotel business. The average for the hotel industry was maybe 40 percent last year, maybe a little bit higher. Sometimes, people will target to recruit from your hotel a department head, because in that department, the loyalty will be to the individual person, not to the organization as a whole. It's very important that when you are taking care of your associates, you're taking care of them in terms of their relationship with their management as well. If that is not a good relationship, again, it's the loyalty to the individual rather than the company as a whole. That's something that we've worked quite hard to improve, and something you should really focus on as well.

The key lesson from loyalty is to trace your company history, go back to how it all began, and let associates feel a part of that. Explain to them how the company evolved, who were the individuals involved, and then relate it to people rather than just the name of a company. Many company names aren't related to the name of the people who began the organization. But if you can do that, that's a very important and very helpful thing to do. It's important as well to put visual images of the senior people in your company around your organization. Then people have a face, a person, to relate to, rather than just a name or a logo.

TAKEAWAYS

- People in China are very loyal and can be very loyal, but more so to individuals than to corporations.

- It's very important when taking care of associates that you take care of their relationship with their management as well.

⊰ Trace your company history back to how it began, and let associates feel a part of it by displaying images of your company's senior people so that employees have a face, a person—rather than just a name or a logo—to relate to.

The Challenge of Self-Expression

Tom Doctoroff

CEO, J. Walter Thompson
for Greater China

THE BIGGEST CHALLENGE in China as a manager is liberating the potential of people in terms of encouraging them, motivating them to express their own ideas. If we don't do that, then things get bogged down in inefficiency and communication breakdowns.

Succeeding in China

Advertising is very abstract. I'm not saying that Chinese people are not abstract thinkers. In fact, they are. Their whole language is incredibly representational, and they are really lateral thinkers. However, it's also a very hierarchical society, where any violation of convention or any rebellion against the norm is something that has always been viewed not just as uncomfortable, but almost as a danger to the established order. So the way that Chinese typically lead businesses is through very rigid structure. Chinese leaders have a tendency to stand up, proclaim themselves the king of the mountain, and make sure that there are power centers underneath them that are competing laterally, as opposed to having any type of challenge for the person that's in charge. Also, the leader can reinforce an overall sense of anxiety by issuing rather nonclear, slightly ambiguous instructions about what it is specifically that he wants.

Now, in some organizations—manufacturing organizations, perhaps—this can be an efficient way to mobilize resources, to

The Challenge of Self-Expression

harness resources, or to rally the troops so that everybody is pointing in the same direction. But in service industries, particularly in advertising, this is pretty much suicidal. Our whole business is based on the easy give-and-take—the flow—of ideas. Nobody ever has completely the right answer.

What you need to do in cultures where ideas count is to create a paradoxical self-expressive environment, where not being self-expressive is dangerous. You need to create an environment where following convention actually is dangerous for any advancement and not expressing a point of view is actively negatively reinforced, in terms of not giving raises, in terms of making sure that people understand that their advancement depends on their ability to stand up and have a point of view.

For example, we brought in a Taiwanese managing director who was accustomed to leading in the traditional Chinese way, which is much more process-driven and control- and command-driven. Within a two-month or three-month period, the entire agency culture started to crack. The efficiency became much poorer. Everything in consulting, advertising, and journalism is about communication, making sure that there are no breakdowns in communication. If people don't feel comfortable in saying, "This is what I think," or "I think that you're wrong because of this," because they're afraid of being chastised by authority, things are going to fall apart very quickly. Taking the opportunity to make sure that expression, and expression of ideas, is the only way for advancement—this is the key lesson of managing in China. As soon as it becomes master-subordinate, you're dead.

Every six months, we have our staff evaluation, where we're having open conversations, and the most important thing in terms of weighting is, does this person have a point of view? Is this person expressing a point of view? If the answer to that is no, any chance of a raise and any chance of moving forward is greatly reduced. And not just that, but even when you're having your brainstorming, you have to bang your fist

The Challenge of Self-Expression

on the table and say, "What is your point of view? Do you agree? Do you not agree?" If you're not encouraging people to express themselves—almost out of fear that if they don't express something, they're going to be embarrassed or lose face—then the whole thing doesn't work.

It's really in the details of every interaction that we cannot underestimate the regimentation that suffuses a Confucian culture like China. You have to create an environment where people know that failure to express oneself is tantamount to failure to career progression. And if there's one thing Chinese want to do, they want to progress in their career.

TAKEAWAYS

⚔ A manager's greatest challenge in China is liberating people's potential in terms of encouraging them, motivating them, to express their own ideas.

⚔ China's is a hierarchical society, where any violation of convention or any rebellion against the norm has always been viewed as not just uncomfortable, but almost as a danger to the established order.

⚔ For service organizations, the key to managing in China is to make sure that self-expression and the expression of ideas are the only means to career advancement.

Extending the Supply Chain

Dr. Victor K. Fung

Group Chairman, Li & Fung Group

ABOUT THREE YEARS AGO, we were looking at the fact that our customers are now requiring Li & Fung to help more in the product development stage. We don't really generate the ideas per se, because that has to be done by our customers with their designers and so on, close to the market. However, we are very much a part of the design process by supporting that. If you have research and development (R & D), we don't do the R, but we certainly do the D.

When a designer gives us a sketch, we concentrate on—within a very short period of time, usually within days—coming back with four different ways of realizing that particular design with different fabrications and with different sets of factories in different parts of the world. Then with that feedback, the designer can say, "Of these four options, I really want to explore this one. Give me more options on this one." In that sense, we're part of the design process.

What we have confronted is the idea of how we put together a product design capability within the whole Li & Fung organization to inculcate that into our own culture and how we then transmit all that into our network of factories around the world. Much of this is in the direction of improved manufacturing practice—better quality, more sustained quality. Increasingly, we're finding that we're really now adding value from the standpoint of design and innovation.

Extending the Supply Chain

Li & Fung used to talk about end-to-end supply chains a lot. Our earlier definition of end-to-end supply chain was from raw material to consumer—all the way from starting with a raw material and then all the way to the consumer. We have now expanded that definition of end-to-end supply chain from *idea* to consumer. There's a piece between the idea that you have and deciding exactly what you want to produce, which is the whole product design stage. As we ourselves develop that product design capability within Li & Fung globally, we're able to share more and more of that with our supplier base, with our partners in this global network. That has helped them also develop, and we're inculcating a lot of those design concepts and design know-how and, indeed, a design culture to the whole thing.

Over time, what we see is that in many countries that we work with, including China, the whole manufacturing base is being upgraded from one of pure contract manufacturing to specification, of OEM, to one that is adding more and more design. We encourage them also to feed into the network by giving us their designs. We will help them improve it and then get that capability marketed properly.

TAKEAWAYS

- ⚑ By extending the supply chain, an organization can capture more business.

- ⚑ Increasing or improving production quality and offering additional services, such as design or development, are examples of adding value within the supply chain.

- ⚑ Incorporating design into the supply chain also allows manufacturers to assist in creating a more successful product for their partners.

Saying Yes to Change

Ying Yeh

*Chairman and President, North Asia
Region, Eastman Kodak Company*

THERE WAS A VERY fashionable saying:
China can say no. Now I tell people, "China
can say no, but Kodak must say yes: we must
say yes to change." We need to also lead the
change, in order for us to be leaders for
another hundred years. It is this generation
of Kodak-ers' responsibility to make sure

that this sustainable growth is laid in a solid foundation during this transformation period.

The biggest challenge we face is not only the mind-set of going from analog to digital, but also more importantly, it's the brand image. Before, Kodak was so closely linked to the yellow box. Now that we're going into the digital arena, we need to find something—a belief, a product, a system— that also represents what Kodak is. At this moment, we're saying not only that we are the house of color, but also that we are the house of a complete image solution. So anything to do with image, color, recording what is happening—communication that relates to your product, or anything you want to report for the generations to remember— you need to come to us. This is easily said, but the real challenge that rests on our shoulders is how we execute it and manage it so this great brand can continue to be what Kodak is all about for another century. We need to use the pride and the history we have, and tell people that since we have written the history, we can rewrite it.

I remember, this was two or three years ago. I was down in Sichuan by a reservoir. I have a vivid memory of an old couple. When you look at their hands, you could tell they were absolutely factory workers. Obviously as an old couple, they are retired, enjoying their retirement on this afternoon outing. The husband was taking a picture of this gorgeous old lady, with the backdrop of the flowing reservoir water. I could see the sun shining on her, her silver hair flying in the air. The instinct is that naturally, they would want to have a picture together. So I went over and asked them if they wanted to have a picture together, could I help them? And they said, sure.

They gave me the camera, and it happened to be a Kodak camera. As a professional disease, I casually asked, "What kind of film do you use?" And that woman turned around. She had been looking at the water, and I said to be careful not to fall off. She turned around, and the look she gave me, in that split second, her eyes said a thousand words. She looked at me—this little bit anger, full of confidence, and this instilled confirmation—to say, "Of course, Kodak. What do you think?!"

In other words, "Don't judge by seeing we are old, retired people," but "Hey, me? Am I going to use anything else? Of course, Kodak."

Even today as I retell this story, I still have goose pimples. And that woman, I have tried to see if I can find her again, because it is that look that gave me the strength and the inspiration and supported my resolve that we can do it—that this brand, this great company, will have a long, glorious journey. And that we will rewrite history.

Saying Yes to Change

TAKEAWAYS

- ⚔ Companies should not only be willing to change, but also be eager to lead the change in order to be successful in the long term.

- ⚔ Established brands need to reinvent themselves in order to address new opportunities and greater expectations in existing markets.

- ⚔ By calling upon its history and listening to its customers, an organization can find the needed inspiration and strength to carry its brands into the future.

⊰ ABOUT THE ⊱
CONTRIBUTORS

Michael Dell is the founder, CEO, and Chairman of Dell, Inc., the direct-sales computer company he founded in 1984. He is also the author of *Direct from Dell: Strategies That Revolutionized an Industry*.

Mr. Dell started his computer company with $1,000 and a goal to build relationships directly with customers. By 1992, he had become the youngest CEO to earn a place among the *Fortune* 500. In 1998, he formed MSD Capital, a private investment firm. In 2001, Dell ranked number one in global market share.

Mr. Dell serves on the Foundation Board of the World Economic Forum and the executive committee of its International Business Council. He is a member of the U.S. Business Council. Mr. Dell also serves on the U.S. President's Council of Advisors on Science and Technology and the Governing Board of the Indian School of Business in Hyderabad, India.

Tom Doctoroff is the CEO of J. Walter Thompson for Greater China. JWT is the "University of Advertising" and the world's fourth-largest advertising agency.

About the Contributors

Mr. Doctoroff was born in Detroit and educated in Chicago. He completed his undergraduate studies at Northwestern University (Evanston, IL) and his MBA at the University of Chicago.

Mr. Doctoroff started his advertising career at Leo Burnett in Chicago but moved to JWT in Chicago. In 1994, he moved to Hong Kong as Regional Business Director for clients such as Pepsi, Philip Morris/Kraft, and Citibank.

In 1998, he landed in China as the Managing Director of JWT Shanghai. In 2002, he was appointed Northeast Asia Area Director (China, Taiwan, Hong Kong, and Korea) and Greater China CEO. Through diversification into customer relationship marketing (CRM) and trade marketing, promotion network management, and brand identity/design, JWT Northeast Asia has emerged as one the most synergistically integrated, creatively dynamic communications networks. Some of JWT China's key clients include Unilever, DeBeers, HSBC, InBev, Ford, B&Q, Perfetti, and Nestlé, as well as several leading local enterprises such as Lenovo, China Unicom, Yili dairy, and Anta shoes.

Mr. Doctoroff is one of Asia's most respected advertising minds. His unique combination of pan-Asian experience, plus more than a decade of work based in China, has made him a leading expert in the cross-border management of brand architecture and brand building.

About the Contributors

He has appeared regularly on CNBC, NBC's *The Today Show*, Bloomberg, and National Public Radio and is frequently featured in publications ranging from the *Financial Times* and *BusinessWeek* to the *Wall Street Journal* and the *New York Times*. Furthermore, he is a sought-after keynote speaker for events such as the International Advertising Association's global symposium, University of Chicago's Global Management Conference, the China Luxury Summit, and the JPMorgan Asia Pacific Equities conference.

Yuehong Fu is the General Manager of Golden Resource New Yansha Mall, the flagship project of the New Yansha Group, a pioneering state-owned company set up by Beijing municipal government and responsible for the operation of state-owned assets primarily in the real estate and retail sectors.

Ms. Fu graduated from the Beijing Technology and Business University, and after earning a degree in economics, she remained in the university's business school for seven years as a respected teacher. In 1992, Ms. Fu entered the shopping center management business as one of the leaders of the Yansha Youyi Shopping City (Yansha Friendship Shopping Center) Group. In 1998, she was sent to the Changchun Charter Shopping Center in the northeastern Chinese city of Jilin as General Manager. In 2000, Ms. Fu returned to Beijing and took on the role of Marketing Director in the Yansha Group and also became the Chinese Director of the Beijing Yansha Center.

About the Contributors

Since 2004, Ms. Fu has served as the General Manager of the Golden Resource New Yansha Mall, China's largest self-contained shopping mall, which claims to be the largest shopping mall in the world. After a series of fact-finding missions to prominent shopping malls throughout North America and Asia, she introduced a number of management best practices into the Chinese retail sector. Ms. Fu managed the transition from planning stages to opening in only one year and, according to New Yansha data, led the mall to profitability after only three years. The Golden Resource Mall has since become a powerful symbol of the evolution of Beijing's retail sector. Among the most prominent of a series of large-scale real estate projects completed in the years leading up to the Beijing Olympics, the Golden Resource Mall is routinely visited by Chinese celebrities and top government officials.

Victor K. Fung is the Group Chairman of the Li & Fung Group, which includes major subsidiaries in trading, distribution, and retailing. Li & Fung is based in China.

Dr. Fung joined Li & Fung Group in 1973 as Manager and became Managing Director of the group's export trading business in 1977. He became Group Managing Director in 1981 and Group Chairman in 1989.

He is a Director of Bank of China (Hong Kong) Limited, Orient Overseas (International) Limited, CapitaLand Limited in Singapore, and Baosteel

About the Contributors

Group Corporation in the People's Republic of China. In addition, he is Vice Chairman of the International Chamber of Commerce, Chairman of the Hong Kong Airport Authority, the Hong Kong University Council, the Greater Pearl River Delta Business Council, and the Hong Kong-Japan Business Co-operation Committee.

He is a member of Chinese People's Political Consultative Conference and the Executive Committee of the Commission on Strategic Development. From 1991 to 2000, he served as Chairman of the Hong Kong Trade Development Council, and from 1996 to 2003, he served as the Hong Kong representative on the APEC Business Advisory Council.

William K. Fung is the Group Managing Director of Li & Fung Limited, one of the largest supply-chain management companies in the world. Li & Fung is based in China.

He is also a Director of various companies within the Li & Fung Group of companies, including publicly listed Convenience Retail Asia Limited and Integrated Distribution Services Group Limited.

In the public-service arena, Dr. Fung has held key positions in major trade and business associations. He is a past Chairman of the Hong Kong General Chamber of Commerce, the Hong Kong Exporters' Association, and the Hong Kong Committee for Pacific Environment Council (PECC). Currently he is a member of the Trade Development Council.

About the Contributors

Dr. Fung is a Director of HSBC Holdings Plc, one of the largest banking and financial services organizations in the world. He is also a Director of CLP Holdings Limited, a leading power company; VTech Holdings Limited, a supplier of corded and cordless telephones and a leading supplier of electronic learning products; and property developer Shui On Land Limited.

Carl H. Hahn is the former President of Volkswagen, Germany. The automobile manufacturer is known for popular models such as the Beetle, as well as today's Jetta and Touareg.

Born into an industrialist family, Mr. Hahn was already connected to the beginnings of automotive engineering in Germany. He studied business administration in Germany, Switzerland, and Great Britain, as well as political science in France. In 1952, he completed his doctorate in Bern.

Dr. Hahn began his professional career in 1953 as Administrator at the European Productivity Agency of the Organization for European Economic Cooperation (OEEC) in Paris. He joined Volkswagen in December 1954. From 1959 to 1964, Mr. Hahn was head of Volkswagen of America. In 1964, he was elected to the board of Volkswagen AG, where he was responsible for the sales department from 1965 onward. From 1973 to 1981, he reorganized the tire manufacturer Conti in Hannover as Chairman, returning to Volkswagen in Wolfsburg as Chairman. Mr. Hahn transformed

About the Contributors

Volkswagen into a global corporation by opening new production plants in China and Eastern and Southern Europe.

In 1993, he became a member of the Board of Directors, which he left in 1997. He is an honorary professor for Industrial Entrepreneur Strategies at the University of Zwickau. In addition, he works in several political, cultural, and social organizations.

Mr. Hahn was awarded honorable degrees by nine universities at home and abroad. Austria, Belgium, Brazil, Italy, Spain, South Africa, Kyrgyzstan, and Germany decorated him with orders. He is an honorary citizen of Wolfsburg, Chemnitz, Zwickau, and Changchun, China. In 1999, he was named one of ten "Corporate America's Outstanding Directors." In 2006, he was included in the European Automotive Hall of Fame.

John Northen is the Area Vice President for South East Asia, responsible for the operational standards and excellence of Marriott International's thirty hotels in his territory.

Mr. Northen joined Marriott in 1986 as a Director of Food and Beverages for Renaissance Hotels in London; assignments in Turkey, Aruba, and Grenada followed. His first posting as a General Manager was in 1993 at the Courtyard by Marriott Royal Leamington Spa in England. Three years later, he was named Director of Operations of the Marriott Forest of Arden Hotel and Country Club in England. He transferred as

About the Contributors

General Manager to the Hurghada Marriott Beach Resort in Egypt in 1998 and, two years later, moved to the Jordan Valley Marriott Resort and Spa, also as General Manager.

In 2002, Mr. Northen's responsibilities were expanded to be the General Manager and Country General Manager for the Marriott Hotels in Jordan at Amman, Petra, and the Jordan Valley. He moved to China in 2004 as General Manager of the JW Marriott Hotel Shanghai and the Marriott Executive Apartments. He was named to his most recent assignment in 2006.

Mr. Northen began his hospitality industry career in 1981 as a management trainee with Sun International in South Africa. A British national, Mr. Northen earned his bachelor of arts degree from Manchester Metropolitan University in 1980. He is a member of the Global Hoteliers Club.

Eric Tarchoune is Managing Director of Dragonfly Group, a consultancy business he founded in 2000.

Prior to founding Dragonfly Group, he held several management positions in China for European businesses in the heavy industry sector, such as Tamrock-Sandvick. He also worked in the light-industry sector for Arc International of France and delved into consulting with Nicholson International in the United Kingdom.

Mr. Tarchoune holds a bachelor of arts in Chinese language and civilization, a master of philosophy in international project management and

About the Contributors

human resources, as well as a degree in international business. He is fluent in Chinese, French, and English. His specialties include human capital and organization management, business intelligence, and knowledge management for foreign companies operating in China. His time in China has given him experience in the installation, development, and restructuring of foreign companies, as well as sourcing and purchasing.

In China, Mr. Tarchoune is a member of the board and former Vice President of the French Chamber of Commerce. He is the founder of Competitive Intelligence and Knowledge Management Working Group of the French Chamber. Mr. Tarchoune frequently speaks at institutions on topics related to his specialties.

Burkhard Welkener is the former Managing Director of Volkswagen Motor Group, the automobile legend responsible for models like the iconic Beetle, as well as more recent successes such as the Jetta and Touareg.

A dedicated learner, Mr. Welkner is a graduate of Braunschweig Technical University, where he studied mechanical engineering, after which he continued to Aachen University, graduating as an industrial engineer. He was also awarded a doctorate in business administration and economics from the University of Giessen.

In 1968, Mr. Welkener began his career at Volkswagen as an unpaid trainee, planning chassis, body parts, and iron castings. By 1970, he was appointed an assistant to the board member for production and quality control. Three years later, he was promoted to Head of Production Coordination. In 1977, he was appointed Head of Controlling and then took over as Head of the Central Production Control Division in 1980. That same year, he was appointed to senior management.

From 1981 through 1988, Mr. Welkener was Head of Executive Organization and Systems, responsible for global organizational structure. In 1988, he moved to Shanghai Volkswagen, where he became Deputy Chairman of the Board. Returning to Germany in 1991, Mr. Welkener held the post of Managing Director of Volkswagen Sachsen GmbH, Mosel. He was then appointed Head of the Braunschweig plant in 1992. Traveling again, this time to South Africa, Mr. Welkener became Technical Director at Volkswagen in Uitenhage. In 1998, the Board of Management commissioned him to create the Polska engine facility in Polkowice, Poland, where he became Managing Director.

Mr. Welkener is the proud recipient of the Bronze Shanghai Magnolia Award, presented by the city's administration. He holds honors from the universities of Shanghai, Magdeburg, and Breslau. He is an Honorary Professor at Tongji University, Shanghai, and Honorary Citizen of the city of Polkowice.

Ying Yeh is the Chairman and President, North Asia Region; President, Business Development,

About the Contributors

Asia Pacific Region; and Vice President for the imaging innovator Eastman Kodak Company.

Ms. Yeh joined Eastman Kodak Company in January 1997 as General Manager for External Affairs and Vice President of the Greater China Region. She was responsible for managing government affairs and public relations for Eastman Kodak's Greater China Region, which includes China, Hong Kong, and Taiwan. She was one of the three members of the core negotiating team that successfully secured approval for Kodak's unprecedented U.S.$1.2 billion project to build China's modern sensitizing industry.

Ms. Yeh's responsibilities were expanded in March 1999, when she was promoted to General Manager, External Affairs and Vice President, Greater Asia Region. On January 1, 2001, Ms. Yeh was also appointed as Vice Chairman, China, to reflect her pivotal role in the execution of Kodak's growth strategy in China, Hong Kong, and Taiwan. On May 9, 2002, the Board of Directors of Eastman Kodak Company elected Ms. Yeh a Vice President of the company.

In April 2004, Ms. Yeh became Chairman, Greater China Region, and in October 2005, she became Chairman and President, North Asia Region. She assumed her current role in December 2007 and is responsible for developing new business opportunities for the company in the region. She is Chairman of Kodak (China) Company Limited, Kodak (China) Investment Company Limited, Kodak (Wuxi) Company Limited, Kodak

About the Contributors

(Shanghai) International Trading Company Limited, and Kodak (Guangzhou) Technology Service Company Limited.

Prior to Kodak, Ms. Yeh had a distinguished career in the U.S. Foreign Service. Ms. Yeh joined the U.S. government in 1970, following a career in Taiwan and Japan as a radio and television journalist, and served as a Political Officer with the U.S. Embassy in Burma and later with the U.S. Consulate General in Hong Kong.

⊰ ACKNOWLEDGMENTS ⊱

First and foremost, a heartfelt thanks goes to all of the executives who have candidly shared their hard-won experience and battle-tested insights for the *Lessons Learned* series.

We also thank IBM for permission to use lessons produced in partnership as part of a series inspired by the IBM Global CEO Study "The Enterprise of the Future." For more information on IBM's market leading series of C-Suite Studies, please visit www.ibm.com/gbs/cxo.

Angelia Herrin at Harvard Business Publishing consistently offered unwavering support, good humor, and counsel from the inception of this ambitious project.

Kathleen Carr, Brian Surette, and David Goehring provided invaluable editorial direction, perspective, and encouragement, particularly for this second series. Many thanks to the entire HBP team of designers, copy editors, and marketing professionals who helped bring this series to life.

Much appreciation goes to Jennifer Lynn and Christopher Benoît for research and diligent attention to detail, and to Roberto de Vicq de Cumptich for his imaginative cover designs.

Finally, thanks to James MacKinnon and the entire 50 Lessons team for their time, effort, and steadfast support of this project.

THE LAST PAGE IS
ONLY THE BEGINNING

Watch Free *Lessons Learned*
Video Interviews and Get Additional Resources

You've just read first-hand accounts from the business
world's top leaders, but the learning doesn't have to
end there. 50 Lessons gives you access to:

**Exclusive videos featuring the leaders
profiled in this book**

**Practical advice for putting their
insights into action**

**Challenging questions that
extend your learning**

FREE ONLINE AT:
www.50lessons.com/china